Advance Praise for *Fling Diction*

"In reading these poems, if you find yourself pulled by the undertow of Cannon's sensuous relationship to the world around them, then know your own appetite will soon enlarge. These poems name the luxuriant grounds by which a self, curious to touch creation, defines itself. Such vulnerability is the hallmark of living. 'Be careful with me,' she says in one poem, 'I'm on the verge of overflowing my own vessel.' Tender, intimate, and unguarded, one easily falls into the gravitational light of her lines."

—MAJOR JACKSON, author of *Razzle Dazzle*, among others

"Frances Cannon's poems are framed closely within her particular, sensual vision of the world. This lens delights in environment: the yawning tongue of orchids, velvet cheeks of lady slippers, sun-bleached exoskeletons of crabs, and cinnamon ferns with sharp teeth. Here, the world is the self, 'blushing and begging to be touched.' These poems are interested in love, friendship, and the continuum of queerness as it leaps from the body to the very landscape. There is a Vermont Dionysian speaker at work, treating herself to soft-serve creemees, and recalling childhood's enthrallments that still seems vividly at work in the adult self. Here, love is about celebrating one another's weirdness, and obsessions, making them into something shared—which is exactly what *Fling Diction*'s poems are: instances of 'mirroring one another's expressions, genders, textures, passions.' In reading these poems we can happily 'grow weird together, singing the same erratic tune.'"

—BIANCA STONE, author of *What is Otherwise Infinite*

"'I need to be swept up and held by arms as solid as the frame of an impenetrable house.'

This is a line from interdisciplinary writer, editor, education and artist, Frances Cannòn's latest work, *Fling Diction*. And though that line is attached to the prose poem, 'A house for Narcissus,' I find myself revisiting that line as a way of anchoring the whole collection in the juxtaposition between being 'swept up' and 'held,' we are with and without in matters of human connection, intimacy and our interconnectedness within nature with Cannon's work and what a ride we are in for! If we even take even part of the title, 'fling,' the word is attached to Old Swedish and connected to 'strike' as well as the other uses that we know of: throwing, hurling all the way to the vernacular related to what we know as a hook-up. Within this collection, we are taken and the words strike our hearts with images that link to our inevitability of fantasy and how it imprints on us like the poem 'Tease' and the way it asks yet dances, 'Let me keep that, at least,' speaking to the hope tethered to a moment. Other work like 'The River Incident,' 'Stories I'm Not Writing,' right until the end with 'While you're away,' take us, sweep and holds us while also casting us away yet tethering us to all of the beautiful complexities that is the heart entangled with bodies that can't help but to also be connected to our natural world. The other jewels within the collection are illustrated across a range of Cannon's controlled poetic skill from every word to every positioning of each verse to the range of form paired with intermittent visual art pieces by Cannon that also tie to another layer that is the beauty of this collection: the danger and the sheer erotism that is nature itself.

Come. Be taken. Be swept up and held by Cannon's latest work."

— SHANTA LEE, author of *Black Metamorphoses*

"What an elegant, hungry gaze Frances Cannon has crafted here! *Fling Diction* is as much a field guide to the natural world as it is an almanac of desire and longing, appetites and threats, unions and reunions. Frances Cannon's poems are precise, wise, and haunting, the self reckoning over and over with self, gender, other, lover– 'someone for whom I am always longing.' I lost myself in these poems and was thrilled to find myself wherever the poems landed me, often swimming, naked, shapeshifting. 'Here, a myriad of alien bodies: chanterelles in the moss, puffballs on a log, and a choir of backlit oyster mushrooms singing their spores into the wind.' Here, poems for finding one's place in the world."

—KERRIN MCCADDEN, author of *American Wake*

"The poems in Frances Cannon's *Fling Diction* move breathlessly through an ever changing landscape of desire. This is a collection suffused with erotic tension, intent observation, and naked honesty. In these poems boundaries of conventional relationships are disrupted and what emerges is a voice ravenous for love, and for pleasure. Here is the vibrant freedom that is found when one is 'without a diagram / for this shifting shape.'"

—ALISON PRINE, author of *Steel*

"Reading Frances Cannon's *Fling Diction*, I kept thinking of Whitman's multitudes. A verdant and hungry queer ecology lives in these pages, and I found myself enchanted by this speaker so determined to experience the world, her brave heart both open and bruised."

—EVE ALEXANDRA, author of *The Drowned Girl*

FLING DICTION

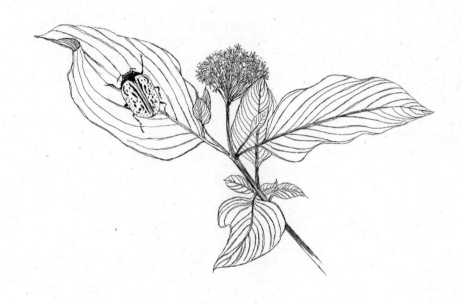

FLING
DICTION

poems

FRANCES CANNON

GREEN WRITERS PRESS | *Brattleboro, Vermont*

Printed in the United States

10 9 8 7 6 5 4 3 2 1

Green Writers Press is a Vermont-based publisher whose mission is to spread a message of hope and renewal through the words and images we publish. Throughout we will adhere to our commitment to preserving and protecting the natural resources of the earth. To that end, a percentage of our proceeds will be donated to environmental activist groups. Green Writers Press gratefully acknowledges support from individual donors, friends, and readers to help support the environment and our publishing initiative.

Giving Voice to Writers & Artists Who Will Make the World a Better Place

Green Writers Press | Brattleboro, Vermont
www.greenwriterspress.com

ISBN: 979-8-9865324-2-4

PRINTED ON RECYCLED PAPER BY BOOKMOBILE.
BASED IN MINNEAPOLIS, MINNESOTA, BOOKMOBILE BEGAN AS A DESIGN AND
TYPESETTING PRODUCTION HOUSE IN 1982 AND STARTED OFFERING PRINT SERVICES IN 1996.
BOOKMOBILE IS RUN ON 100% WIND- AND SOLAR-POWERED CLEAN ENERGY.

What lips my lips have kissed, and where, and why . . .

—EDNA ST. VINCENT MILLAY, *Second April*

She felt something close to exhilaration, of a kind that people can permit themselves when they are blessed with love.

—TOVE JANSSON, *Fair Play*

CONTENTS

Fling

Bruises form in the dark

Brood

Little owl

Circe

A new leaf

Fling

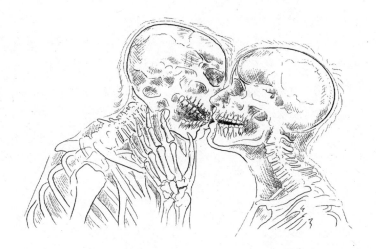

A house for Narcissus

How much of homosexuality is narcissism? —Susan Sontag

My words stumble over the fat tongue that squats heavy in its cave. Are her thighs as milk as her neck that bends and curls so taut in the half-light? She's more woman than I am. I need to be swept up and held by arms as solid as the frame of an impenetrable house. A thick house that locks me in so that I look out at all of the women with milk necks and breasts like mine and wonder if I would feel as happy as a man to taste this woman's nipple. I break the house and burn the frame and eat the ashes. I chase a supple form from afar and wish to hold that pale chin so sharp in my palm. I turn to kiss its lips and find my face pursed in its place. I am small, shivering so little for a big house.

My woman arrives at the costume ball dressed as me. She blushes with stolen red cheeks that she peeled from my face. As she lifts her sleeves I see my tattoos upside-down on her inner forearms: fork, knife, spoon, rabbit. We waltz with gin feet and kiss dark in an upstairs space. Her red dots transfer like two thumbprints smudged to my skin. She asks in a lull, *what's it like to kiss yourself?* Now I am sick from liquid excess and spinning head, straining to see; black air obscures the impression of her features in my pillow.

Objects of desire

To be queer
is to find sex appeal
in stones placed *just so*
between two white granite slabs
on a trail to Hunger Mountain,

in the knots of trees
shaped like imprints of peach pits—
hollow caves of wood-flesh,
layers framed by scar tissue
and rough bark lips,

in the folds
of ill-fitting garments,
where stitched ribs overlap
and rub the skin here, and here,

in the yolk, which breaks
and spreads—before my spoon
can slurp it up, down the sides
of sourdough, blanketing
each green leaf, filling
the space between crumb
and plate, so that I must lick
the golden pool when all else
has been consumed.

Wild orchids

The spring brings yellow lady slipper orchids,
fleeting beauties, rare to discover in mud season.

These flowers make me think of the two of you—
the gaiety of their attire, costumed blooms scattered
through the floodplain forest, their erotic poise,
their jubilance and humor. I envision Llyr's pompadour,
finger-combed casually to one side; Emma's perpetual smile.
I can almost feel my arms draped over each of your shoulders
on the couch in your living room, all of the dogs curled
like living pillows on our laps and at our feet.

The orchids say, "come closer, pay a visit,
touch my lips, peer into my bowl." They catch
and hold the sun like dozens of miniature lanterns
dotting the green underbrush. These golden orbs
have an animal quality—their mouths gape open to reveal
stripes of red spots; each mouth features an upper lip,
a round protuberance, clitoral and gleaming.
Two magenta tendrils spiral out from either side
of the floral orifice; red silk scarves twisting in the wind.
One larger petal rises skyward from the center, a yawning tongue.

I stare into the face of one lady slipper and recall our kiss
shared three ways after a dance party in the Upper Valley,
all the way down in Bethel, Vermont; odd place for queers like us
to congregate; we were all so desperate for touch
after the long hibernation. Bounce and sweat,
bubbly pét-nat and an oyster platter,

the caress of a velvet cheek in the dark,
so many hands and mouths together in one bed.

After the long winter shadows, this is all so fresh—
ephemeral blossoms, fiddleheads and ramps;
new morning glory sprouts pop up each time it rains;
grass grows faster than the blade can catch.
You are both new to me, too. I hope this lasts
longer than the season of the wild orchid.

She wants

To put on her warmest clothes: handknit wool socks,
long johns, and her old hand-me-down cashmere sweater.
She wants to skate across the frozen pond to the sea caves,
slick with moss and mottled with orange lichen,
then back in the company of her crush, who will carry
the heavy thermos of tea, and who will help her lace
and unlace her skates. Later, by a wood stove or fireplace,
she wants to be wrapped in warm blankets, layer by layer,
then unwrapped all at once; her crush has an appetite
that translates to speed, like tearing through the crust
of sourdough bread to get to the airy sponge within.
Under the wool, her crush might find a few layers of silk,
or nothing at all—only skin, blushing and begging to be touched.

Déjà vu

We must have met before—

Perhaps I saw you somewhere a decade ago,
that summer I spent in San Francisco, living
with my uncles near the Castro. They often
brought me along to bear bars and drag shows;
I was their little tagalong niece, not related by blood,
but through literature, queerness, and happenstance.

Once, the hairier uncle joined me on Wednesday night
at the Amnesia Bar for beer and free jazz. We watched
the Lindy Hoppers, and I shared a few dizzying spins
with handsome strangers, more my uncle's type than mine.

He asked, "Why don't you ever go to the Last Call Bar,
on 18th street, that's where the lesbians are.
This place," he paused to gesture around
at the swing-dancers, "It's too straight for you."
We left the cozy pub and he walked me to the corner
of the Last Call, grinning like a father
dropping his daughter off at her first school dance.

I entered, alone, watchful. The bar was tight
and lit only by neon signs. Peanuts on the floor,
pool table as centerpiece, jukebox in the back.
Didn't I see you at the table by the window, waiting
for your friend, perhaps, to order another round of drinks,
or waiting for me? I didn't stay long enough to find out.

Or, maybe it was in New York, the summer I stayed in Manhattan
with my three friends who studied at the Art Students League.

We took mushrooms in Central Park and tried to sketch
one another's portraits, but Caleb's face kept melting
in my vision and my pen wouldn't cooperate, so we climbed
trees and stared down at strangers on the park benches.
when our brains sorted themselves out and objects
began to re-align, the trio of artist friends ordered takeout
and got into bed together, and I went to the MOMA.

Colors and shapes still throbbed, and I found myself stuck
in front of a Giacometti drawing; his figures are already
out of whack, limbs protruding and necks elongating
in all directions. I turned my head from the sketch
and saw you standing several paintings to my right—
at least I think it must have been you, though
I didn't know you then—you stood with your hands
in your pockets and your head tilted toward a Miró.
Knowing what I know now, I wish I had approached you,
asked your opinion, asked you out for a coffee, and more.

Or, perhaps I met you at the flea market in Paris, "Les Puces,"
when I lived in the blue apartment of my grandmother's
former student, on the fourth floor of a narrow tenement
in the third arrondissement. I was so lonely that summer,
and I tried to walk it off all over the city, to leave my
solitude behind on the cobblestones like mud or gum.

I walked in so many circles around Les Puces
that I lost my sense of direction somewhere in the heart
of the market. Didn't I see you there, holding an old silk
handkerchief up to your eyes, inspecting the embroidery?
Didn't you look up then, and recognize me from somewhere
in your own past? Haven't we played this game before?

Beauty's Luncheonette

Montreal, 2022—yet Nat King Cole still croons
"Unforgettable" in this bright hive of a diner,
a time capsule of colors, textures and smells.
The servers' costumes may not have changed since 1942—
all women with short-cropped hair or long, tight braids,
black eyeliner and powder-blue smocks.
Finger-sized maple syrup bottles stand guard
behind the counter, nestled in with old milkshake mixers,
cocoa tins, honey jars and milk-glass mugs in pastel colors.
The white honeycomb floor tiles crawl with a pattern
of black and blue fleur-de-lis. The giant neon-green clock
above the entrance tells me it's 9 am this February morning,
the day after a winter squall that smothered
all of the cars and bicycles in deep snow.

This is also the morning after a sweet kiss with someone new.
She's a petite tattooed lady, mother of a tailless cat,
collector of antiques, Jewish, cynical, overflowing with stories
and puns, born and raised in this Canadian town.
I am dining alone today, but I can't contain
a painfully broad grin and small eruptions of delight,
all of which must reveal to the patrons of this diner,
strangers all, my secret infatuation.

My eyes drift and rest on two androgynous queers
in matching black hoodies and candy-colored tuques
sitting in the corner booth, their faces half-bathed

in the bright sun streaming in through the floor-to-ceiling windows.
They could be twins, but the way they stroke
each other's knuckles tells otherwise.

I return my gaze to my plate—a mess of egg yolk and sesame seeds,
the remains of a lox and cheese bagel breakfast.
I may either melt into the table into a puddle
as bright and liquid as this yolk, or bubble
over the lip of my mug with giddy joy, spilling onto the tiles
to intermingle with half a century of black coffee stains
and road salt. Be careful with me,
I'm on the verge of overflowing my own vessel.

Word appreciation at the art museum

I visit Montreal's Museum of Fine Arts
alone on a Tuesday during an April snowstorm.
An installation of wall-to-wall oil pastel murals
by a contemporary painter, Nicolas Party,
occupies the upper floor, featuring
partly-rotten-yet-still-erotic fruit,
women with pissed-off expressions,
androgynous bodies with beetles and worms
adorning their flesh, and tall, skeletal red trees
puncturing serene landscapes and icy pools.

These lurid, sensual figures are enchanting,
but the focal point of my attention centers on
the label of an old painting from the permanent collection
by Frans Snyders, Antwerp, 1657. The title itself
could be a poem, or the first sentence of a gothic novel,

> *Still Life with Game Suspended on Hooks,*
> *a Lobster on a Porcelain Plate,*
> *a Basket of Apples, Plums, and Other Fruit*
> *on a Partly Draped Table with Two Monkeys*

Why did Frans decide that whether or not the table
was fully or partly draped was as important
as the presence of two live monkeys
and the corpse of a partly disemboweled deer on a hook?
How did he select these particular fruits to pair
with lobster, and why no mention of the artichokes?

I would love to read the notebooks of this Frans Snyder,
to see the drafts of titles that he may have written in ink
with a quill, versions of lists describing the scene,

> *Still Life with two wild monkeys*
> *wreaking havoc on the dinner table*
> *Still Life with a string of tiny dead birds*
> *and two adolescent deer near an open window*
> *Still life with grapes and raw meat*

Oh, to have been a fly on the wall
as Frans strolled through the markets of Antwerp,
selecting produce to put in his basket, or arriving home
holding a cage with two chained monkeys
and describing to his wife, mistress, or assistant
his vision for a new painting. "I think I'll arrange
the game on a circular hook, hanging above a bowl
of fruit, and I'll set the monkeys free on the table,
to eat and explore while I sketch…"

Did he imagine that one day a woman would stand
in front of his painting on a cold day in Canada,
writing a poem inspired by his title?

Ruelle

When a bicycle skids to avoid a staircase
on l'avenue de Lorimier in Montreal,
both objects vibrate with the tension
of proximity.

Above the church of Saint-Enfant Jesus,
attic dancers twist in pockets of air,
a protective film just beyond the skin.
They respond to force: magnetic, gravitational,
the pull of warm body towards warm body.

Two Southern expatriates, old friends—
one with loud hair and a pinstripe dance-suit,
the other a carpenter who swam across the border—
advance with wordless nostalgia to the center of a crowd.
They invoke their old Cajun home by shuffling
side-by-side to a two-step waltz.

When a woman approaches a man on a balcony
three stories up, he tells her the word for this alleyway
is *ruelle* in French. She notices his angled teeth.
She deliberates by pointing out Orion and the dipper.

As two tongues advance, both tremble and tighten,
arching stiffly like cats in the face of danger.
When objects make contact, they merge
like two drops of liquid on the lip of a metal railing.
Together, the droplets slip and descend.

On trying to draw a portrait of a lover from memory

Sketch

The lines in my drawing blur as the palm of my hand
drags across the page, smudging and rearranging pencil marks
with sweat and dust. It's a hot, wet summer, and simple tasks
take on the quality of honey—slow, yet infused with light.
My lover's form morphs as I add and erase; is this line straight
or curved? How long are their lashes? How robust are their lips?

I've had more time on my hands since I quit my teaching job,
to wade through the swamp of my own thoughts
to read, draw, and contemplate books that I want to write.
One manuscript I'll never publish: an illustrated catalog
of every person I have ever loved. It would take too long,
expose too many secrets, scratch old wounds.

I'm reading the memoir of a bisexual woman, Jen Winston,
who wants to reclaim the pejoratives "greedy" and "confused;"
concepts often thrown at people like me
who demand too much from life. Appetite—
is that such a sin? The only confusion I've felt
is why everyone else would limit themselves
to loving one gender or one person.

Research

A woman catches my eye at the Wallflower Collective,
a local bar that hosts a monthly dyke night.
In Vermont, these queer gatherings

are few and far between, and I chase them
with a near-religious fervor. I like the way
this woman holds her round, glinting mouth
with a fierce elegance, turned slightly down
at the corners as a challenge to the world,
as if to say, "what do you want?" or "so what?"
I gather my strength and ask for her number.

A week passes; I arrive early for our first date
at a brewery overlooking the lake.
I realize with regret that I have chosen a very
heteronormative crowd for our first conversation:
beer and bros, overpriced gastropub fries.
She arrives and we fall into our own private black hole,
loving to hate on academia, hating that we love academia,
two burned-out nerds seeking employment in new fields.

When it comes time to kiss, I feel the straps of her bra and pause—
does this masc-presenting, self-identified butch,
on the spectrum towards nonbinary or trans male,
want to diminish or celebrate their breasts' existence?
I can switch to either mode of appreciation,
and have loved partners transitioning beyond
their feminine parts, lovers who have built new parts
to fit their chosen gender, as well as women proud
of the anatomy indicative of the sex
they were assigned at birth: the whole range
from sculpted tits to tender scars to cis-boobs.
I need more information: I ask my date
to send me their master's thesis,
and I end our date early to read the PDF.

Text and image

The paper circles around the experience
of "black butch trans women." In other words,
had I mistakenly assumed that my date, attending
dyke night, had been a cis butch lesbian,
who might have wanted to bind or hide her breasts,
yet in this case, her breasts are new, chosen,
but not to be flaunted? The lines blur.

I turn from reading the PDF to my sketchbook,
where I draw a portrait of myself and this date
as David Bowie and Grace Jones, based on a photo
of the two androgynous, pansexual superstars
in Paris in 1983. Their styles and faces
are beyond gender: Bowie with his platinum blonde
pillow of hair and sharp jaw, Jones with her high
cheekbones and head-to-toe leather outfit;
she even wears leather gloves, reaching across
Bowie's waist to pose for the photo, her arm
parallel to his belt, suggestive, possessive, bold.
In my drawing, I am a female Bowie, and who
is she? An androgynous Jones—my drawing
can't capture the strength of her face.

Body versus mind

I set the drawing aside and retire to bed
with the company of the book on my nightstand,
borrowed from a lover, "J," who sits squarely between genders:
Macho Sluts, written in 1988 in the heyday of butch lesbianism,

before the author, Pat Califia, transitioned to male.
Nothing like outdated gay literary porn to fall asleep to.

When I close my eyes, I remember when J held me down
like a bird trapped indoors—tenderly assertive,
my wings pinned at my sides to restrict flight or fear.
In the height of this delicious tension, they paused to ask,
"Do you like my gender expression?" I had already answered
their question with my body, but they needed the verbal seal;
we must feel seen to access our desire, to feel safe in our lust.
In spite of their dominant grip, J felt vulnerable to my gaze.
With my 'yes,' the game resumed, my little bird's heart
fluttered wildly in the grip of their strong, firm hands.

J is a master of touch; they know how to give just enough,
and no more. It is this nuanced confidence that attracts me,
yet there is a disconnect between their physical conviction
and their self-perception. We once spent a dreamy afternoon
cooking congee bowls with jammy soft-boiled eggs, white pepper,
steamed eggplant, toasted sesame seeds, and while the rice
simmered on the stove, we explored each other, leaning against
the kitchen counter. The next day, J texted, "do I kiss
in a gendered manner?" It is as though J's body performs
separately from their mind. The former dances, while the latter
pulls back to watch from the shadows, questioning everything.

Utopia

In my dream, I introduce my father to all of my lovers.
It is a reunion, of sorts, uniting my blood and chosen family.
The man with whom I share a home shows up to this gathering

with another woman—he carries her on his shoulders like a child.
Nobody's body is static, everyone's form shifts continually.
Height, gender, sex, age—swapping, transforming at a rapid pace.

I wake with the sense that we have all made peace—
family tension, interpersonal drama, doubts about our own bodies—
these complications slip away like skin shed from a snake,
leaving only the naked, pure essence of each being.

Honey Hollow

It's been a week, or three—checking off tasks,
phone calls with my boss, conversations
with my family about queer allyship or lack thereof,
discussions with my partner about polyamory and autonomy—
I'll admit, there's a continuous low hum
that vibrates beneath it all: the shape of you,
the way you press into me, mold me like butter.

Take me back to Honey Hollow,
the narrow river valley in the shadow
of Camel's Hump Mountain. Let's bushwhack
through patches of sensitive fern,
swap ghost tales, flirt sideways
as we crisscross down the steep, muddy bank,
gasp at the sight of the granite slabs
rubbed smooth by the pounding water,
marvel at the ribs and mounds
of blushing red quartz. We'll kiss, there,
and my feet will slip on the wet moss.

Let me guide your hands
along the routes of my desire—
you'll stop just short of the places
I want to be touched—your approach
liquifies me; we fall together and apart
in waves of movement; bring me closer.

Your hands in my hair, pulling my strings
this way and that; I'm yours to choreograph.
Let me explore the contrast between the delicate line-work
of tattoos crawling up your neck and the ridges
of scar tissue along your ribs, my hands on your chest,
reading the braille of your skin. I haven't slept well
since that day—I'm distracted, replaying our dance
like a film on loop. Release me from this erotic insomnia,
take me back to the water, give me something tangible
to break this spell. More than your words,
I need the warmth of your flesh.

Sofia

Sofia from Seattle, Atlanta, San Francisco—poet,
pole-dancer, boldest flirt in the workshop,
with copper strings woven into your black hair
and papayas printed on your blouse—of course I wanted
to invite you in; I felt the end of the trip looming.
What a relief when you finally kissed me
after seven days of teasing,
on my final night in the city of roses.
We hid in plain sight
from the other night-owl writers
who drifted to their rooms
after the dance. We hid in each-others' mouths,
on the bridge above the duckpond,
under the waxing gibbous moon.
I wanted to invite you in, but I know the taste
of these fierce, flash loves that turn bitter quick.

Fling diction

I'm in bed with an editor
I met at a writers' conference.
I dream that her four lost teeth
speak to me from the hallowed ground
of the softball fields of her youth.

When I wake to tell her of this vision
of her teeth animated in the dirt,
she corrects me—the details of my dream–
Rugby. Softball is too cliche.
I broke my teeth playing rugby.

I refrain from describing
my half-written poems
to her, O editor-muse;
those which began,

      Let me list the ways . . .
      Things I would like to do to you . . .
These phrases devolve as I bob between sleep
and waking, but the sentiments remain
as the morning light shifts from red
to mustard yellow, then to a weak tea,
let's say chamomile—unless that's too common
an herb, in which case forget the color.

I want her to hold me in the sheets
while I go hunting for her teeth, to walk
back to the spot where her preteen face
was high-tackled into the sod and sparse grass.
I will mop the blood from her jaw with my shirt,

pick up the pieces of bone and carry them home,
massage her kneecap back in place, and kiss
away the grass stains from her shins.

I tell her: look, the light in the curtains
is turning white. *Off-white*, she says.
Eggshell white. Bone white.
It's time to get up. The light is white.

Tease

A new-old friend joins me on the dance floor;
we've circled one another in the neighborhood
for years, always one degree of separation
in the queer community of a small Vermont city.
They strip off their winter layers, all the way down
to their white crop-top muscle-tee, and they waste no time
grinding down to low squats and twisting flashy shapes
with their long, taut limbs. I can't help but watch,
bouncing distractedly in their shadow, admiring
and, privately, desiring to touch their waist.
They dance circles around me and the circles shrink,
bringing their skin within inches of mine. I'm either
shy or cautious, so I resist the urge to reach out
and close the gap. Later, on my solo walk home
at morning's two or three, I send a text asking
for clarity—and their response is one of surprise:
Who, me? Flirt? No, you must have imagined it.
Perhaps I've conjured this erotic sprite; created them
from thin air; perhaps they don't even exist. I'll choose
to keep my version of reality: I prefer the rapid heartbeat,
the sweat on my temples, the proximity of their body,
the mirage of intimacy. Let me keep that, at least.

Delicata

Sunday afternoon, we rest by a pond
whose murk hides a dozen koi. I am a visitor,
a city interloper, a hired hand, a friend to the man
beside me who runs the farm. The small of my back
presses against the wood of this sagging bench,
and below, the dog digs herself a dirt pit to stay cool,
panting as she settles in beneath two sunburned humans.
The man lights a pipe. We add heat to our already
steaming forms: fire herbs, hot coffee from a cup
balanced between our hips. The sun's fingers
tattoo our legs in tiger stripes.

Ribbons of muscle along my spine hum like violin strings,
singing the day's work: hurling gourds from the far field
into the bed of a tractor, twisting, bending, and wrenching
delicata from the tangle of vines to hurl them skyward.
One after another, from my hand, to his hand, then dropped
into a mound of its kin—so many cousins, striped green
and pale yellow, some with red-tinted faces, some speckled
from a lifetime in partial shade. And the pumpkins—
the weight of each orb lingers in my wrists; the effort
of lifting and throwing these ribbed, slick-skinned babes
tallied in my ligaments: one, two, three, four, five, start again.

My thighs, curled over this bench, remember the form
held between. The grip of longing, the tension poised
like a catapult bent towards the earth, the spring of release
which leaves them quivering. Here I am again in the field:
my spine, the squash, the toss, the catch—those hands
receive my weight. I toss, release, and we are suspended,

waiting. I squint to watch a ribbon of sweat drip down
between his ribs, caught in the trap of hair
above his belly button—violin strings ring
with the memory of that salt.

Disappearing objects

Don't look at your hands while juggling;
they should appear blurred, gesticulating skyward
as if rearranging the heavens. The Pleiades constellation
disappears the longer you stare.

If you're after a lucid dream, study your hands
in the daytime; memorize their warmth,
arrange each finger's position. In sleep they flicker,
drained of color and temperature,
but if you hold them steady
they'll follow you through the night.

You grow accustomed to the habits of a body.
His lower lip bitten in concentration, his eager feet.
When you squint, shadows under his chin, nose, and brow
separate from three planes of light: forehead
like a plum freshly polished by shirtsleeve,
and two cheeks singing under a lamp.

Behind eyelids, you see your hands
on the concave plane below his ribs,
imprinted in reverse color like the after-image
of a bulb. In the body's absence, the vision of skin
pulses and fades.

Theories of non-attachment

He permits her to stroke the arch of his foot
with a pencil while he reclines on a bed
of palette boards and black rabbit fur,
reading Kant with his eyebrows gabled
like dormer windows.

She may pinch his thumb while they march
across the Williamsburg bridge,
but she may not hold his elbow with her arm.

Blindfolded, she may smell his bottled oils:
essence of pepper for the wrists,
agar wood for the neck, vetiver
for the temples, but she may not kiss
his wrists, neck, or temples
until after dinner.

She may ask for lessons in unicycling,
speculative realism, banjo plucking, tattooing,
or Bagua martial arts, but she may not
mention the painted nude
hanging from his doorframe.

Watching the market man juice a ginger root,
devouring scallion pancakes at the wonton shop,
he tells her not to hope for more
than accidental overlaps of their desire:
finding synchrony in breath and step,
succumbing to blindness by sunlight.

Cosmopolitan swine

At the art museum I stare
down the nostrils of a golden sow.
She bares her teeth and tongue so wide
I could climb in, or at least place a hand
between her gilded jaws.

The image of her snout follows me
as I chew my way through the farmers' market.
Spoon after spoon of goat cheese,
several toothpicks of salami, a pastry
from every pop-up bakery, a pickled egg.

I feel the fangs of the golden pig
sink in, inch by inch,
and in turn, I grow
my own snout, teeth.
My belly sags and I drag twelve
shimmering teats along the sidewalk.

Asleep on a log, I dream of sex

I skinny dip with two men in the lake.
They call after me as I swim into the deep,
as though I might drift into a hidden cove
and leave them to fend for themselves
in the wilderness.

Back on the red rocks, we share slices
of cold steak cut with my pocketknife.
In the past month, they have each tried
and failed to take me to bed—I let them each
take a kiss and nothing more.

Today, I walk down the beach in search
of a shadow to nap in, far enough away
that the men will not be tempted
to transfer their lust to my shape.

I fall asleep on a log with a slim book of poems
over my face. Ants crisscross under my skirt
and I dream of a long line of men bearing gifts:
one man, a carpenter-ballerina of my past affections,
offers a gold ring in a scratched glass box.
We tangle on a futon, he drives away,
and I sell the ring to a pawn shop.

I wake to find that my legs have splayed on either side
of the log as though I have melted in the sun.
My swimming companions have disappeared.

I treat myself to a soft-serve creemee
from a roadside stand called Fun Crest,
where the tap water tastes of dead frogs
and an old, toad-like couple sells bucketfuls of worms,
miniature flags, and cans of gasoline like souvenirs.

Pickleweed

Salicornia pacifica

We enter the salt marsh with fingers crossed
for flicker feathers and chanterelles.
The hillside provides bones: a clean spine, intact,
a doe skull with a green map etched on her temples
like pathways on a molded topographic globe.
We lose our shoes to the bowels of the pickleweed carpet—
one breathing, gurgling mass of beaded glasswort,
sandfire—little red-tipped fingers clutching digested crabs
the size of spiders, whose sun-bleached exoskeletons
glimmer against the dull palate of the estuary.
A chorus of marbled godwits chant *kow-eto*
kow-eto as they lift collectively into the fog.
The flag woven of their wings pulses a few beats and fades.

Pursuit of a tiger

Catnip

Can I lure a tiger with catnip, tempt
an apex predator with this old wives' weed,
trap megafauna with domestic flora?

A cousin of mint, they called it cat bait.
They used this herb to lure feral cats into cages
to be shipped off to the pound. Farmwives
would twist the cats' necks
and toss them behind woodsheds.

Catnip proliferated in medieval garden beds.
They grew this mint to repel bubonic rats
and draw in cats to kill the rats, but the cats
came instead to sniff and lick and chew,

to slink between the thyme and sage, to rub
and bruise the leaves, to steal the mint's scent,
crushing and killing the plant to revel
in its ephemeral perfume.

Domestication zodiac

All my lovers have been tigers. They were born
in the Chinese lunar year of the fire tiger.
I dream of a tiger who lives in a glass palace

on a winter beach. We make love, the tiger
and I, but are arrested by forest rangers
for bestiality and smoking forbidden leaves
in a public botanical garden. I dream of a tiger

who hunts my family under an apocalyptic moon.
I dream of a tiger who crawls behind me
under a quilt the size of a valley,
until I emerge and leap upon the lump
of the tiger's form and stomp him to death
with my feet, as though I were stomping grapes,
but the grapes are his offal which oozes
out from a rip in the quilt and saturate
the fibers of the cloth.

I am infatuated with a tiger: a woman born
in the year of this zodiac beast. She is far
away and won't commit. She has too many
other lovers and the miles between
us translate into days, weeks of silence.

I long to tame her, bit by bit,
to establish a mutual need
between beast and master.

Wind

Before the scientific revolution, a cleric
named Topsell, who wrote of gulons,
dragons, libbards, and fairies in his bestiary,

believed all tigers to be female. They
"engender in copulation with the wind."

The day my tiger escaped, when I lost the hunt,
a homeless fiddler sang for me
an old Swedish ballad about a man
who fell in love with a woman
made of wind—he couldn't pin her down
or keep her for his own, for how can one
hold onto wind, trap a tiger, tame a beast?

Recipe

Having no wind up my sleeve, I'll tempt
my tigress with catnip—intoxicate her
with the tender spring shoots of my rough-
stemmed mint.

The neighborhood cats come from all around
to roll and chew my mint: an ash-gray cat
with only one eye, a cat with burrs and twigs
stuck in its fur, a cat with one black paw and no tail.
They roll head-over-tail and rub their bodies in the dirt.

As a tea, the mint has a sedative effect:
two tablespoons of dried catnip, boiling water,
a spoonful of honey. An herb to seduce and sedate.

Come to my garden, tiger, take my bait.

Uranian fruit

A form shifts in my dreams
from woman to man and back,
or it is formless, a being
with neither name nor shape.

Plato wrote about Uranian love,
a noble lust for the souls of young men.
He praised Aphrodite—born to a sexless planet.

This is a weightless love, like hovering
in the lake over a lionfish
that I am drawn to and also afraid
to approach, so I float and stare
until my fingers turn to prunes.

She tries on a jacket to see if it fits.
She passes for a gentleman.
I am she, for her, I am hers, I'll be hers.

Madras and plain color button-downs—no frills.
Streamlined. Amber earrings shimmer from her lobes.
Her jaw is angled like the chins of the porcelain dolls
I boycotted as a young tomboygirl.

She tells me, *I don't consider myself a woman*
but the body as such does fine work
moving me through the world.

She brews me coffee, a courting dance.
I will call her any name she chooses.

I dream of fruits sliced open to reveal fibrous hearts
and oval rows of seeds in slippery purses:
papaya, cantaloupe, peach, guava, pomegranate,
served to me on pewter breakfast platters
by bare-breasted goddesses of Creole folklore.

I spend all Sunday fretting over dinner
for the object of my newfound infatuation.
Here we are, naked, on a sheepskin rug,
in front of the fireplace.

Her question triggers my subconscious fruits:
Would you still want me if I were a man?

With a start I realize we are nude,
and I am without a diagram
for this shifting shape.

Yes, and in my saying so, she transforms:
I will love him, if he lets me.
I dream of fruit, sliced in half,
exposed, gleaming, raw.

Epistle

For Jack, after Proulx, Wilde, Woolf

When I pause on the gravel road,
clutch your forearm with my hand,
exclaim in a half-sigh, *Look at the moon!*
when I wax poetic over an egg yolk,

or write to you of the fireflies
which accent the night-dark lilac bushes,
I mean to write, remember when

we were cowboys together,
kicking our boots in the sagebrush
to scare off rattlers, tossing
in our sleep to keep the mice
from making nests of our collarbones?

Remember when our wives
caught us kissing in the doorway,
when we could only touch
in the valley between blue mountains,

when we dodged tire irons
and fists in rodeo parking lots,
when a single sweet glance
tossed us into the line of fire?

Remember when I was the king of epigrams,
and you, the object of my Uranian adoration,
like Socrates and his budding protégés,

you were my golden lady boy,
my high society side-dish,
my companion in salons and shadow dens,

and your father, the Marquess of Queensberry,
left a calling card accusing me of sodomy,
and I was punished for merely loving you?

Remember when we were two Victorian ladies,
married, with children, but both restless
and lusting for adventure?

and we would write to one another
from steamships and garden terraces
about architecture and literary criticism?

In every line of poetry about the markets of Tehran
or about keeping house, we meant to write,

I want you here in my lap, for our bodies to merge,
and for the morning to stretch
beyond the limitations of clocks.

Bruises form in the dark

Private

The nose of her black Cadillac
blocks a private footpath that cuts
through a field, past a marsh
guarded by cottonwood trees,
through a grove of maple saplings
to the stone-lined lip of the lake.

Several time zones apart, two bodies
simultaneously breathe the same dream
of skin on skin and wake sweating
in a stripe of light: for her, a streetlamp,
for him, the moon. In the desert, a little girl

builds a playhouse out of tumbleweeds.
She cuts through the school grounds
where the neighbor boy pushes her against brick
and spits down her skirt.

A note on the windshield of the Cadillac
warns: *you are trespassing, go away.*
The girl watches her naked mother jump
from a railroad bridge. The railroad leads
to a wild strawberry patch where geese
chase toads into a ditch. As the sun sets

a spot of red rips through a veil of gray
and expands. Two figures wade
up to their waists in wet black.

Beware the birds

A woman, alone, on a business trip in a tropical city,
walks back to her hotel after dark. She calls her sister
who is snowed in up north during the second bomb cyclone
of the season.

How's my dog?

Good, but she got into the Easter chocolates.
Oh. Did you hear that Amy's grandma died today?

Shit. Should we postpone her birthday party?
I already put the cake in the freezer for later.

Their conversation dissolves when the woman
spots a solitary pelican perched on a rotting wooden post
in the middle of the river, his bald head and withered gullet
illuminated by a crimson river lamp, nearly motionless
until he spots what might be a fish or another morsel
of bloated bread, then he dives deep, emerges with empty beak,
and returns to his throne to wait; hunter of the swamp,
guardian of the under-bridge, gatekeeper to the red-light district
of night-bird-life. The bird dives again and hops back
to his post, the fin of a herring flapping out of his beak.
His leather neck-pouch quivers with fish death, and a vision
of shadow men visits the woman's peripheral delirium—

Men in the dark, under the bridge, in the bush, men
in cloaks, with knives—the pelican swallows
and the woman sucks on the names of men
from books—Mr. Hyde, Dorian Gray,
Faustus, Bluebeard, Jean-Baptiste Grenouille.
The man in her mind transforms into a swan

and she stands naked as Leda at the water's edge.
Her sister calls out through the phone
                    Frances Frances

until a white, flat-faced owl splits the night sky
in two and disappears under the bridge,
disrupting the dark, oiled surface of her trance.

Pounce

There's a man who often crosses my path
when I'm out in the country, alone.
He doesn't belong to anyone.

He takes different forms, slipping
from suit to suit depending on the day
of the week, his mood, the weather.

One September day, I pulled off a gravel road
onto a stranger's lawn for a tag sale en route
from one swimming hole to another. The man

approached me from behind—I *felt* him
before I saw his shadow. I was flipping
through picture frames, 25 cents each,
some empty and some still hugging the ghosts
of a child's pastel or pressed flowers.

"Some good stuff here for a little homemaker.
You live in the neighborhood?" He wore a hat
whose rim obscured the upper half of his face,
and he leaned forward in a looming curve
as though to wrap his bulk around the small scene
of me: my body, my little mutt tugging on her leash,
the box of frames, the tag sale, the bend in the road.

Another day, another road, another skin suit,
I found him leaning against his car as I came down
from the mountain still calling my dog's name,

whistling every other breath, cawing
that high-pitched tune which pulls her
from her squirrel-hunting mission. The man

didn't blink or smile or nod as I approached,
though I mumbled an explanation for all the noise
I made, hollering after my beast. Finally, he broke
the spell of his own face to say,

"We all get lost now and then"—my cue
to turn back to the woods to lose myself
as far from this man as the hunt
for my dog could take me, and *fast*.

At night, alone in my cabin on a hill,
where the only evening sounds are owl chatter,
crickets, and every so often, a bear,
I heard the man's motorcycle pull off the road.
His engine growled all the way up my long driveway,
lights off, and I knew it was him, even through this black,
shapeless disguise, this shadow-costume, dribbling oil
on my land, his machine lurching and shuddering
like a boar hungry for a sow's heat.

Then—silence. Engine off. A battle of wills:
I *dared* him to dismount. I had my hand
reaching to the knife drawer, claws curled to dig at eyes,
knees aimed to thrust, and the greatest weapon
a woman can wield—*fear*, which she keeps at her breast,
all of her days, on every bend of every road,
poised to shapeshift into wrath.

Stories I'm not writing

After reading Carmen Maria Machado's In the Dreamhouse

Perhaps it's time I write about all of the scary stories
I've lived through, the love-turned-horror stories:

Nick, who—long after we broke up—threw stones at my window
and threatened to kill my new lover
with his bare hands.

Ben, who abandoned me in Guatemala City
after I refused to sleep with him;
he bought a motorcycle and disappeared
without a goodbye.

Mario, who left me alone for days at a time
in a dirt-floor shack in Santa Ana, and when he returned,
he turned me into his housewife—the kind of housewife
the man ignores until dinner is on the table.

Sam, who showed up drunk to my book launch and flirted
with all the women in the room, then made me drive him to a party,
and then to an all-night diner for an early morning snack,
and when we finally returned to his trailer on the farm,
he refused to look at me or touch me,
even though we shared a bed.

Maybe I haven't written these stories yet
because it feels more sustainable
to write about something else,

anything else.

The river incident

There are two sides to this story: what really happened,
and what could have happened. The young woman
fell in love with her English teacher: handsome, charming,
blue-eyed, rugged yet intellectual man from Montana.
She became his star student; aced all tests, wrote long
and compelling essays and book reports, but she didn't
show off or raise her hand in class. She felt his approval,
from his inviting smile when she entered the room
and his compliments in the margins of her papers.
Once, they walked together to lunch, but separated
when they reached the cafeteria. Once, he asked her
to babysit, and she examined every inch of his home.
Once, during a free period, they left campus
and went fly-fishing in the Passumpsic river
with his old black Lab. He loaned her a pair
of rubber gaiters so that she could stand in deeper water,
but there was a leak in the heel, and the river crept in
until the gaiters filled to the brim. The river swept her
into the current, and the old dog swam in after her,
pawing uselessly at her feet. The man grabbed her shirt
to pull her back. She heard the seam rip at her shoulder
but it held long enough to lead her to the shore.
What might have happened then between them,
reunited on land—a story to tell or to hide, a story
to make her blush or cry or rub on her pillow at night,
a story to spread around school, a story which gets him fired.
None of that. Instead, he gifted her his old Volvo,
his fishing car, with hooks in the dashboard and mud
in the footwells. The car broke down two weeks later,
she graduated, and her family scattered to new towns.

Her teacher moved into her old family home
with his wife and kids. Everyone is too busy these days
to reach out. Nobody talks about what could have happened,
what nearly did, at least not out loud.

An altar for fish and bird

As guests at their wedding,
we should be giddy and lightly bubbling
in the presence of their affection.

Our rash—not of blood or flesh,
but a flare-up of tension—
feeds on fermented nectar
and spreads to our necks
in the golden tent,

a loud and hot bruise
for me to hide within the folds
of my skin-tinted silk.

I wander down along the lake,
facing away but not far apart
from your heavy gait.

At the water, a throbbing swarm
of hot bodies calls me to their light
under the ceremonial arch.

During the day, this archway had framed
a bird that flew with a dead fish
trapped soundly in its beak.

Now all is black but for the candles
that flicker around the base of the altar,
the bodies reflecting the flames,
and a swath of stars whose constellations

cast the blurred reflection of a city
onto the surface of the lake.

A song built from drunken
harmonies undulates in the throats
of several nude bridesmaids
like the amorous breathing
of an intoxicated beast.

I hunger to curl into sleep
on the bosom of this song,
to feel my cheek rising and falling
on its skin as I had when my mother
read by the lamp too long into the night.

You carry me limp and unwilling,
a wriggling fish in your beak
along the open corridor
of carnival tents to our own #5,

through the flap to the twin beds
which had, in a much simpler hour,
been pushed together
for the sake of our unsteady union.

Withdrawal

I saw you today and craved sugar. Most mornings
I wake with the taste of dream-cakes
thick on the roof of my mouth:
flourless tortes that suffocate butter knives,
cloud waffles layered with Chantilly cream.

You, under whose watch I feared to laugh,
who pulled so many curtains of salt
from beneath my lids, who bared your teeth
after a drink. You still make me hungry.

In a dream you sneak into my bed
and stay there till morning. My mother chides:
don't let rats in the house, they eat the bread
and leave us nothing for dinner.

My bed becomes a loaf; cotton and springs
turn to sponge and crust. The loaf
disassembles itself: flour, water, salt—
four corners melt into soft white.
A rat in my bed, a rat in the flour,
a dark blemish on sheets of pure grain.

In the bakeshop I dip my hands into a barrel of flour.
I withdraw my fingers: bleeding, bitten, and sweet.

The seventh season

Flood

She finds him sitting outside the night cafe
dressed in the skin of a coyote.
He whispers a soft song as if his voice
were wind through wheat.
The tune breaks the dam she built to keep him out.

Coyote

Hard to hide in a room full of eyes.
Hard to hush in a raucous stew of voices.
She runs herself into a wall of bushes,
pushes her chest up against a fence.
Here he is, spitting laughter from his muzzle.
She shouts a whispered plea into his stone face,
Get back, beast. Get down.

Vessel

She wakes alone in a house that contains her like a ship
in a day so dense with rain she will not see land
even if she stands on the deck, braced against the slick posts
with a telescope pressed flush against her waking brow.
She looks for him in the shadows of the pantry
and listens for him when the rain thickens
on her roof, yet she will not step from this ship
to be folded into his sheets of gray.

Drone

After his call, she buries the phone
in the dog's jaw to see it be slobbered on and crunched.
She coughs away the coming sobs.

She wrenches the phone in twists
like a soiled cloth in need of wringing.

She slips the phone between the lips
of her mattress to smother its incessant whine.
She dreams of the sound of bees drowning
in a vat of honey for the stiff, pearl-white blossoms
below the viscous sweet.

Wheat

This is the fourth and final time.
She will enter determined
and he will flare up
or turn down the folds of his lips
and the slick orbs of his eyes
will pull at the thick fabric
of her steadfast refusal.
The sack that holds her in place will rip
and she will tumble like so many grains of wheat
into his eternally upturned palms.

Hunter

She bikes a wide loop
away from her usual route
to avoid passing his house.
Four blocks too far north,
seven blocks too far west.

Spinning around a corner she feels him
crouching like the shadow of a hound
panting in the matted roots of a cedar hedge.

He wouldn't have seen her
through all the rain, although
he had been waiting, searching.

Litter

He feeds the season a letter a day,
slipping them into the fickle wind.
He stuffs his love into the crevices of autumn
and she whirls the letters with her foot
on the way to the lake. The envelopes gather
in the gutter with the faded leaves, growing mildew
and melting into the dormant city gardens.

She perches on a stump at the lake's edge
to tell her dog the story of the seventh season.
The mutt coughs up a letter through ink-stained fangs.

How to peel an orange with a broken wing

Pack your leather boots and plan to drive seven hours to kiss
a woman who tastes of brandied cherries and cream;
she has a bed for you in Brooklyn. Pack your paper and ink,
your Victorian novels, and a list of two dozen restaurants
intended to make you drool and weep.

Before you leave, crash your bike and land on your chin.
Land with the full weight of this month's rain flung above you
as you balance on the tip of your face with the finesse
of an acrobat. Feel the gravel grate your jawbone.
Stain your dress with blood, thick as oil paint,
and walk to the nearest familiar house.

Here is your ex-lover's apartment. Knock on his door
and ask to bloody his towels with your new red paint.
Dip your head into his bathroom sink while he watches.
Roar from your gut like a beast giving birth. Rattle his dishes.

Here you are in the mirror with a blood goatee.
Here you are with a patch of facial hair that drips down
your collarbone and swells like a bulbous blue tuber.

At the hospital they will give you a smile made of tape
and decorate your chin with a cotton pom-pom.
They will glue your wounds and send you home with a broken wing
like a crow that mistook a windowpane for a tunnel of flight.

Here, at home, your dinner is one yellow pill and an orange
that you pierce with your left thumb. You peel its skin
in small bits that fall like the scales of a fish to the floor.

Brood

Anna

If you are having a bad day, or if you
have been having a bad day every day
for the past three years,

drive an hour out of the city to an old quarry
that has grown over time
into a cold, clear blue pond. Meet your friend
at the trailhead, let her soothe you
with small talk, and together you can
ease into deeper waters: your failed career,
her divorce, real estate, eating disorders,
psychopathic ex-lovers, sinus infections,
sex toys, lust and longing.

Lay side by side on a shared towel
under the partial shade of a wild cherry tree.
No other humans can be seen. Strip down
and swim, exultant, howling both at the bite
of the cold water and at the animal joy
that rises in your throat.

Leave bad days behind
like an oily film on the pond's surface.
Emerge whole, clean, shivering naked
like a newborn in the hungry sunlight.

Moving through the rooms

On

My stepfather huffs the mantra of the meadowlark
and knocks ash from his sweetgrass into a bowl of dirt
as the women rub smoke into the walls clockwise.

For a week after his blessing, we taste ancestral breath
in our roasted butternuts and candy-stripe roots.
The women subconsciously drift clockwise.

In a month, three unexpected visitors will appear after dusk.
Sideways rain will lick away our papers;
a hurricane will inhale chairs from our porch.
The women's blood will synchronize.

Off

Moths make their way into the cupboard
and weave lace garments of oats and rye.

Rub the oil in, pull the dough until it grows thin.
Hold it up to the light, see the translucent skin rip.

My body doesn't fit; I pinch my flesh
seeking the source of battle cries echoing from my gut.

Bicycle dismount: my woolen dress splits at the hip.
I trace circles into the pavement a league beneath the crows.

In

The colors of hours blend to a dull gray
which sticks to my teeth and cannot be swept from the carpet.

Are these men interchangeable? Which face, thrust, or vocal gesture
will linger as a trapped shadow in my sheets? Each one flits
like a moth from a jar when I lift the lid.

No trace of warmth in the palm, the bed is carefully tucked,
no crumbs remain on my plate.

A spoon on my tongue, please.
I want a visible impression of weight on the pillow.

Out

Lightning casts secondary shadows of five nude figures
onto the rippled page of a lake. The bodies quiver
in shallow water like birch poles stripped of bark,
pale arrows shot from the cliff into silt.

We tear bread in small, violent gestures
and wear vermillion waxcaps behind our ears
in autumn's absence of blossoms.

With

Mother, draped on her chair like damp laundry, her limbs bruised
from my verbal assault—raises her book as a shield
and flips pages and sucks thick air.

I throw a wordball at my mother's face. She hides the ball,
crushes it, shakes it, swallows it. I open my face
for her to return the blow, but she will not budge.

My tongue twists in the milk glove residue of lukewarm coffee.
Tongue encased in white, and I writhe in a tube of wool.
When I blink I see snakes rubbing against cottonwood bark
and sandstone, shrugging off old skin.

Without

The orange berries of the Chinese lantern plant—
relative of tomatillo and ground cherry—
shrivel within their veined cages.

The women hang bouquets of twigs around the house
mourning the color that slips from the mint above the stove.

Swallows build tenements of mud in the eaves
and settle into a season of hunger.

Reunion

A father figure comes to visit. I haven't seen him in ten years.
What do I call him; my ex-step-dad? Former father? Friend
or foe? I don't know of any archetypes for stepfathers
in fairy tales and myths; perhaps Claudius,
but he's more of an uncle figure. Evil stepmothers abound,
while the men and their lies and lust slip through the cracks,
blameless and nursing their own wounds, while the women
swoon, fight, bleed, beg, marry, bear children and die.

He arrives in his classic Ojibwe style; long graying hair, bandana,
and beaded vest, bearing sweetgrass, smiles and hugs—
what can I do but accept, while my small-talk tongue retreats,
hiding dumb and limp behind my teeth. My mother glows,
ebullient; why? How? It feels like yesterday that I pulled her sleeve
towards land and safety while she leaned towards the cliff—
metaphorically and literally 'on the edge' after this man's
betrayal. My sister and I nursed her back to relative sanity,
and now I see no traces of trepidation or rage lingering
in her beaming features. I've lost my appetite. Cheers,
to everyone at this reunion potluck; welcome back
"Dad," to the bosom of our family. Apparently,
the past and all of the memories buried within
have evaporated for everyone but me.

Yet, he has grown older, and something about his
gradual loss of hearing and sight renders his person
sympathetic; my grudge softens around the edges,
blurs in and out of view. He cranes his ear towards
the kernel of conversation, and spends too many minutes
showing photos from his phone in the middle of dinner:

his infant grandson, the wildlife in his backyard, pictures
of his paintings and the exterior of his house in Montana.

I take note that not once during his visit does he ask
any questions about our lives, our well-being, health,
partners, work, life, art—except about my dog,
who is an easily accessible surface topic.

We take him on a tour of our Vermont: to the lake,
to the apple trees, to the pebble beach and maple creemee
stand, where he asks Mom to take his picture with the ice cream,
and I wonder, *for whom?* Does he have a new love to send
selfies and sweet nothings to? Will he break her heart and home?
If not now, when, and how badly?

Finally, back in my mom's kitchen, I crack—quickly and entirely
open, all over the countertop—an inarticulate hot mess.
I tell him all of the reasons this small talk is impossible:
his lies, his infidelity, his absence. He swallows and nods,
and for the first time on this trip, he asks me a question:
"What can I do to make this better?"

I don't have an answer, not yet, and even if I did—
he might not be ready to listen.

Anatomy of a lavender wand

The play breaks for intermission. Gray heads pour like marbles from an old tin into the lobby. Grandma Helen fell asleep halfway through the act of—Fiddler on the Roof? Little Shop of Horrors? Mozart's Requiem Mass? Our fingers bleed from handling sewing needles and crochet hooks in the dark. I dig her out of a mound of lavender buds and tear through a cocoon of wool and ribbons with my teeth. Once she has risen, we walk arm in arm down the aisle, but she begins to shrink and wobble until she is a wooden marionette, limbs dangling from my fingers. We push through the bodies in the lobby towards dusk. I fight through a swarm of locusts towards a bench on the bank of the Great Salt Lake—all we want is to sit down, to rest, but the bench-ladder towers high above the buoyant water. I heave the weight of two beings rung by rung to the top where I lift Helen—now a little boy who scrapes his knees and weeps, now a sick rabbit—into my lap, and feed her lettuce into the morning while salt drops from our eyes into the lake.

Eve

On the afternoon before Grandmother Helen's scheduled surgery—
an emergency procedure to save her spinal column from collapsing
in on itself, her vertebrae melting and crumbing, not even steel rods
can hold her together—when she should have been
bedridden, strapped down, drugged, perhaps—Helen insists
on spending the day in her garden. She can't walk anymore,
but she forces a limping shuffle around the house, and when
in the yard, she hobbles and lurches over stones, dragging feet
through dirt and moss, leaning when she's able on trees
and branches for support, like some wayward scarecrow

haunted by a wind-spirit, moving ever so slightly this way
and that, lighter than a tumbleweed, built of old straw,
held together by a thin, patchwork cloth that catches
on thorns and bears the scars of time: stitches and edges
frayed. Oh, scarecrow Helen, you've done your work,
stood your ground, guarded your home from shadow-birds
and bad omens, rest easy now in the herb garden,
take a seat by the lavender beds. Your straw is coming apart.

The surgery looms overhead. It obscures the light,
casts a blue-gray hue over her flowers, blurs
her vision of the pruning shears in her bony fingers.
Snip it away, trim the blight, toss the rotten leaves in the compost.

She shall *not* be deterred. Her garden *will* thrive. The sorrel
overflows the old, sagging wood of the raised bed—vivacious
greens with a taste of bitter lemon. She leans to pluck the bud
of a lavender blossom, and some plane within her tilts,

as a spinning top, towards the end of its whirling, slows
into a wobble, bending and dipping towards the tabletop.
Helen falls in the garden and breaks her hip. Tomorrow,

they will cut into her neck, just below her brain,
fusing the bone of her skull to the bone of her spine,
and why not add the hip while you're at it, doctors—
two snips for the price of one; she's broken
in so many places now, perhaps you can weave
a strong and steady thread from head to toe.
Be quick, be nimble, she's a delicate wisp
of a woman, and she has letters to write, books
to read, dogs to spoil, and a garden to tend.

Translation

My father emails me from the opposite coast
with dream transcriptions several times a week.
As soon as he wakes up each morning,
he uses voice-to-text on his phone
to capture the dreams before they evaporate
into the heat of the day. In one, he balances
on a tricycle along the precipice overlooking
a deep river. He holds his dog in his arms
as he pedals to safety. On the other side,
he steals the blanket from a sleeping baby
in a bassinet so that he can wrap his cold,
frightened pup in warm cloth.

These dream emails are long, detailed, and usually
too odd to decipher, but this week's dream sends me
all the way back to the first home in my early days,
to the house in the avenues where we hunted slugs
in the poppy beds and threw a mattress on the stairs
to slide down into the basement, where a giant stuffed bear
kept my sister and me company at night.

We made an appearance in my father's dream:
my sister joined him on a camping trip
as his wilderness adventure side-kick,
and I stayed behind, sulking, alone.
His email reads, "she wrote in one of her journals
that she needed to get away from me and get
off on her own—she needs more song and poetry."

These days, sensitive critters abound in my house—
my dog howls her mournful blues when the sirens pass;
my man cries as he reads comics to his kid on the couch;
I sit in the yard and scribble poems and aspirations.
My father has never been vocal
about his emotional inner workings—
this is how he communicates his affection:
a digital translation of his subconscious.
I can finally see that he understands me.

Spring cleaning

My sister rolls her rug halfway,
like a blintz unraveling on her plate.
The rug offers a new playground for the cat;
let us review our grade school prepositions:
       kitten on a half-rolled rug,
       kitten across,
           above,
   near,
           beneath,
   upon,
           kitten within a rug.
My sister cuts my hair—our lifelong tradition—
while the record skipps and my tea grows cold
on the mantle. Snip, snip, and now I am shorn.
We rearrange our bodies and homes
piece by piece in anticipation of spring.
Although it is still shivering weather,
we plant pepper and tomato seeds
and push the winter socks
to the back of the drawer.
Nearly bald, I'm ready
for a new season.

Little owl

The spill

We're hooked on fluttering. We flail our limbs
around the room like fledgling birds
stIll learning where to put our wings,
or beetles flipped on our backs,
spinning our legs in the air—
our mutual excitability is a danger
to all open containers—we knock our drinks
to the floor, bathing our feet in foam.
We don't mind, we're just biding time
until the dancing begins.

Will all this buzzing stave off sleep? It's creeping
up on me, at the lids—I blink it away and sweep
the spill up and out of sight. You say,
"Goodbye summertime sadness,"
I say, "Please, winter, wait a while."

We slip out the side door of the bar—
still daytime, to our relief—and lean back
into the sole growing shadow
to watch the baby parade. Little sprouts,
learning to hold their skulls up on elastic necks.
Young velvet hounds, tripping over their own
oversized paws. All the young boys
thrust their teeth into bowls of fried meats,
their fingers snatch at slivers of cheese.

What will happen to our appetites, come equinox?
Will the frost cure us of these urges? I don't want
to let the salt slip from our skin. Can we keep it,
thick and glistening, at least until the sun tucks
herself in for the night?

Nesting

After we thumb the last of the golden raisins
and kolach crumbs from the plate, after we lick
these thumbs clean of butter, let me fit my body
around yours like the fattest Russian nesting doll,
soup spoon to your teaspoon. You fit around
the smallest doll—the spoon-body of my dog.
She curls into the little bowl of space between your chin
and your thighs, pressing nose to neck, eyelashes
slowly knitting together. Her legs chase
phantom rabbits through the underbrush. I stand
on the border of sleep watching you follow her
down the path. Your limbs twitch in time to her paws,
two creatures leaping just out of my reach.

My dog begins to whimper, and then a soft,
low howl rises in her throat, muffled by the pillow.
She has lost sight of her prey—a flash of white fur
dives into the shadowed brambles—or she hears me
singing from far away, through the trees, through the sheets
of my bed, through the tremors of your body.

Your fingers tap my arm one-by-one
as though in sleep you have transformed me
into an instrument—your saxophone,
the one which in waking life sits untouched
in your mudroom. These dream fingers climb
up and down my skin, pulsing with song. I hum
a parallel tune which traces the vision
of a dog and girl running after rabbits
in a winter marsh.

Teeth

I sat down to write about your mouth, but you wouldn't stop
moving it—your mouth—I tried to get a good, hard look,
like the drawings I make of all those faces in motion
which I sketch in secret on trains, buses, and planes—
the old men asleep with mouths agape, drooling
on their cable knit turtlenecks, men whose traps snap shut
as they leave their dreams behind, to find me staring,
my pen cross-hatching the details of their intimate sleep,
or the dogs whose profiles beg to be rendered in my notebook,
but they won't settle down—trotting in tight circles
in their nests of blankets. Your mouth is in motion.
At least with words I can pin down its essence—
if not the image of your mouth, I can write about how you lick
the tip of your pen to draw out the ink when it sticks,
and how your lips curl inwards when you concentrate,
and those teeth—sculpted throughout adolescence
by a set of wires, and your lips, still moving—
I think I'll stop trying to write about your mouth and just kiss it.

Masquerade

Little owl with pockets of shadow for eyes,
you look as though you'll break if I touch you—
don't cry. Only an hour ago you were flitting
through the crowd at the masquerade, torn
between which of your loves to dance with and when,
with the upper half of your face hiding
behind a feathered mask. When I tried to kiss you,
your beak bit blood from my lip. I left you alone
with the woman in silk—the water nymph in a mer-skirt.
I thought that's who you wanted, but I found you, much later,
wandering alone in the night—circling my house,
stretching your wings, your eyes dripping black.

Word trade

Our overlap is rare, these days—
Five years ago, we would write together
every week, and kiss, and dance. Now,
we have our own homes and new lovers,
and the closest to a kiss we get
is sharing this juice you brought as a gift.

We rest under a tree and trade words
as prompts for future poems.
You give me *petrichor*; I can taste and smell it,
metallic and dusty, with a hint of sweetness.
I give you three words—a code for my secret desire:
   space, parallel, longing.
This is the way two poets talk about love.
What I wish I could say is: I hold a space
for you—not a placeholder, you're not
 a backup plan, rather, a parallel love,
someone for whom I am always longing.

We are a puzzle, you and I, never clear
nor straight, twisted in knots old and new.
You speak to me about the weather—
the thin sliver of moon or how many
winter layers you're wearing—I ask
how you've been and you say, "like an alien,"
or "surviving"—you ask about my home life
and I shrug the question away.
There is a language humming between us,
shouting affection and rage. One day,
we'll share this conversation out loud.

Bittersweet vine

How can I explain? Take this image: today,
during a windstorm just before the rain hit,
outside my kitchen window tendrils of bittersweet vines
appeared frantic, reaching for a branch to cling to.

Bittersweet is a climbing vine, invasive in Vermont,
always twisting around a borrowed stalk,
tree branch, or fencepost towards the sun.
These tender shoots extend into the void
of inclement weather, longing for contact
and finding none. If I'm the vine,
you're the absence of a tangible surface,
an invisible temptation. Yes, my roots
have a strong base, my thick and sturdy arms
are protected by a rough, woody bark,
and if need be, my little green tips can twist on themselves
for stability, but they'll continue to seek connection,
tossed by the wind, stretching outwards in vain.

Autumn cravings

I kept opening myself for you over and over
like some ill-timed clam, oblivious to the tides.
Exhausted by the motion, I closed for a while,
distracted myself with mundane tasks:
gave the dog a pedicure, chased dust bunnies around
the legs of the furniture, caught crickets for the frog.

When you knocked again, I couldn't help it,
I flung all my doors and windows
wide open to the breezes.

A hike, a picnic, a nap by the beaver pond;
I said yes to it all. We found a mushroom
in the woods with a soft white skin
that peeled easily off to reveal
a dense, translucent orb like an eyeball.

While you bathed your feet in the cold river
and wrote in your poetry notebook, I examined
a rock which appeared to have two breasts
as flat as mine had been throughout
my twenties. This rock, partly submerged
in the water, bared its two little stone nubs
up towards the sun and air, exposed.

Overhead, a solitary branch of red leaves
swayed on an otherwise green maple tree,
and all around, the smell of sweet cinnamon.
I spoke to you about all of my cravings:
warm apple cobbler with vanilla ice cream,
to kiss you, to open again and let you in.

Sagittaria

Here is the spot where I once found an adolescent sturgeon
floating tranquil and unperturbed just above the lake floor.
A hoard of little children flocked to me when they heard
my exclamations of awe. They wanted to touch
its moldy spine. I remember wondering to myself
how a fish so small and young could look so old.
I feel that way sometimes—prematurely wrinkled,
slow, and weary of the day's repetitions.

This is the place where we came to talk
after my faux pas. I came prepared with a speech,
to apologize and explain, but all I could do was cry
and say "um," silence, "um," and you responded
with half a dozen shrugs, squinting against the sun.
Two poets, inarticulate together, in desire and rage.

We didn't get far in our conversation—
both exhausted by this cyclical argument,
turning round and round as slow
as the sturgeon in shallow water.

Tired of talking, we took our clothes off and swam
in broad daylight, just far enough away
from the families building sandcastles
and the condos with floor-to-ceiling windows.

We felt invisible to the public eye if we stayed underwater,
but we could see each other, slightly distorted in the waves,
and we could see the mergansers, cormorants, and even a hawk,
or maybe it was a kestrel, so small and sharp.

We walked as far as we could through shallow waters
to where the sand sloped down to a deeper blue,
around the slate cliffs, to a place where we thought
we could be alone.

Someone is always watching—this time
it was a man—smoking, fishing, and napping
between two boulders. When I saw him,
I covered myself, while you smiled and stretched;
I gained confidence through your gestures.

I know I shouldn't have said it, I shouldn't have told you
that I wanted to kiss you, we've already been through this.
Ours is a story that fades and resurfaces every season.

Here I am again, alone. The Sagittaria flowers have washed up
on the shore, arrowhead leaves and tendrils in tangled nests,
white blossoms smelling of September rot.

Circe

Matryoshka morning

Today, my thoughts are Russian nesting dolls—
parallel images, similar shapes, in different sizes:

My crush on a woman with lips chapped from smiling too wide, Sa.,
who writes poems during work and hides them in her pockets.
This love nests within a late-night conversation I had with her friend,
P., the singer with ever-blushing cheeks and a collection of costume jewelry,
who fell for her grade-school English teacher twenty years her senior, L.,
who taught her the difference between writing love songs
and writing songs for love.

The story of the forbidden love of P. and L.
nests within the novel I'm reading, Murakami's *Sputnik Sweetheart*,
in which an elementary school teacher, K.,
pines after his friend, a young Japanese woman, Su.—
an aspiring novelist who smokes two packs of Marlboros a day
but never finishes a manuscript. Su. becomes infatuated
with a Korean woman twenty years her senior, M.—
a classical pianist-turned-business-woman,
who buys Su. a new wardrobe, takes her out to fancy dinners,
and orders whole bottles of the finest wines, which they never finish.
M. convinces Su. to quit her career in writing
and work instead as her personal secretary.

Su. learns that there's a delicate bone in the inner ear of lesbians
which makes them genetically predisposed to same-sex attraction.
She's afraid to learn the shape of her inner-ear bone.

This novel's plot nests within my own winter affair, now dissolved,
with a Russian woman twenty years my senior, O., a radiologist

with early childhood trauma—no father, absent mother,
and the homophobia of the Soviet fist she grew up under—
she grew a taste for fine spirits and traveled the world
climbing mountains and sailing lesser-known coves.
She bought me a new wardrobe and took me out
for prix fixe dinners which began with oysters,
peaked with some slow-roasted beast, ended
with sorbet. And—a new wine with every dish.
O. tried to convince me to quit my teaching job
and work instead as her personal secretary.
I packed up and left when she started making
verbal lists of my neuroses. This, coming from
a woman who can't even mention her mother
without cringing like an injured dog.

All winter long, I had been
the small wooden doll
nesting in the center
of her big Matryoshka house.

The outer shells have now been lifted, one by one,
and I'm fitting my shape into new forms,
new nests, layering thoughts and loves
and novels into dolls with new faces.

Offering

Take this bite of buttered polenta bread
from between my thumb and forefinger.
Don't be too precise—if you slip
and catch a bit of my skin with
your lips, we can try again.

Let me rub eucalyptus and mint
into the small of your back, and wipe
the sweat with a blue towel, or two.

I may not articulate, in words,
my appetites or affections,
but I will peel the spongy flesh
from every slice of this pomelo
to feed you piece-by-piece.

I will sprinkle catnip tenderly
around the paws of your Mushka,
the beast with a low-hanging belly.

I will turn down the edges
of your bedsheets, slap air
back into the pillows,
and place them side-by-side.

History of the safety pin

My body is a ribbon of white and red silk, your body
is a needle of iron and bone. My middle coils,

producing tension. I open with a spring-like action. You,
with deliberate wide-eyed wistfulness, you

do as you are told. You shed your skin
in the history of politeness.

If I am sick, I am rehearsing death. Either
I am being evicted or I am under attack.
Can we be alone together, below incandescent fruit,
in a strange paradise of flesh and stone?

At noon, we stumble upon great joy,
an accident of proximity.

My body is a list of constituent elements,
a measurement of worth.

My boat rises in your parlor. Let me in at high tide.

O

At first, my life with her was thrilling: the abundance
of her wealth, the late-night dinners and wine pours
of early courtship, the strength of her hands
directing my movement in the dark
of her room. If I had stayed with her
for a few more months, or years—
I would have become her little housewife,
just as she suggested. She wanted me to bear her children;
she froze her own eggs and looked to my womb as the vessel.
She scorned my ambition and rolled her eyes at my daily efforts;
teaching, she said, was *a waste of time*. I began to believe
her. My work was futile next to hers: as a doctor, she saved lives.
If I had stayed with her, she would have succeeded in molding me
to her shape. Every day we spent together dissolved a layer
of my conviction; I kept quiet, nodded along to her words.
Once, she latched her mouth to my neck, leech-like;
I wore the bruise for a week, hidden under turtlenecks and scarves.
What violence was she capable of? If I had stayed any longer—

After the affair

I want to pluck you,
wet, wriggling trout and lick
the blood from your pierced lip.
I'll release you only if you swim back
upstream during my season of want
against the current which tempts you
towards unknown oceans. Let me be
those waters. Let me be your unknowing,
your undoing.

When my eyes sag
halfway down my face,
tie them back with string.
Try plastering them in place.
I trust the tools you wield
more than my own. Rebuild me
again and again, dismantle me,
rebuild me.

My body machine sends me
illegible signals of craving
and hurt, on the hour every hour,
as I drift and push my limbs
through air thick as spit.

Taurus

Twelve months have passed since you made us dance topless
in your basement theater. You decorated our faces
with veils of soiled teabags and black lace.

Do your eyes still burn with Oakland teargas
that you drank like nectar, that you welcomed
into your tattooed embrace?

Are your lips as red as the blood that rises
in the groins of your dozen suitors?
And my favorite mole, is it still there?

Are you still with that boy that stole you from our living room,
the one who dresses in burlap sacks
and eats only out of trash cans?

The one who placed a cow bone in my toilet,
who arranged two naked dolls in a knot of copulation
on my kitchen table for my mother to discover?

The one who rode a mechanical rocking horse
around the house and kissed my dog with open lips?

Does he make love to you with the same nihilist fury
that drives him to spit urine down the world's throat?

Does he still dangle tin, twine, and doll heads
from his fingers and call it art?

I used to watch you paint faceless forms
with translucent skin and paper bags for heads,

appliances with vibrant organs,
greyhounds with rows of nipples like teeth
and so many legs they can't walk.

Is the typewriter still whining, purring, clicking
its tongue in your lap? I timed my breath
to the beat of your poems in order to sleep.

The machine followed in a leather suitcase
wherever you went. To the Mustache Ball,
where you spoke through a pair of deer jawbones,

to the night cafe, where you poured hot toddies
and gimlets to bearded trolls,

to Brooklyn, where you crouched on the subway
floor chewing your own existentialist haikus
and spit them out in a vertebrae pattern on the cement.

Do you still carry a whiskey flask in your breast pocket
for the hour when you need to growl destruction at the snowbanks,
smash glass against brick and drum wooden spoons
on someone else's thigh until you draw blood?

Do you still moan ghost songs into the hollow cavity
of your banjo, and pin cloth roses into your bed-spring hair?

You made us dangle paper birds from wires
above your hunched back as you spit
like Baba Yaga into the crowd.

You made us cry into teapots and toasters
while you flickered your pearl lampshade
from center stage and hammered a slab of meat
until it fell limp to the dirt floor.

Will you write to me
before you trigger the Apocalypse?

A new leaf

A dance for alchemy

She seeks a simple life: roasted rice tea, flowers
and herbs drying on the windowsill. She is as fragile
as these specimens: thin as leaves of labrador tea,
brittle like dried blossoms of yarrow.

She dances to turn the wood beneath her feet gold,
the oat grass in her hands gold, the gaslamp gold.
She makes her body into wind, to pass between
ghosts of her mother's furniture.
She darts her head left and right,
imitating the young doe she envies.

She makes her body into a knot, then rips
the knot, hurling herself through the ceiling.
Thoughts of middle life swallow her insides. She is hollow
and floats from the breakfast deck into the marsh,
catching Spanish moss on her limbs. In the morning
they find her transformed into the husk of a dried bay nut,
washed up by the new moon tide onto Limantour Beach.

Glutton for sunlight

We spread our picnic around, stretched it out
in various wild places throughout the day—
First, on the upturned root ball of a silver maple
bent precariously over the backwater swamp,
where the night heron watched our slow luncheon unfold—

Then, to the private beach of Charlotte where non-residents
like us must pay to enter and abide by the interminable
list of restrictions: no swimming, no smoking, no fires,
no dogs, beware of zebra mussels. We snuck in our mutt,
I took off my pants, and we made out under the rock ledge.
I could hear the voice of the town sheriff in my head,
"No sex, no nudity, no rock collecting,
no natural beach behavior..."

We took our next picnic to the top of Ethan Allen Hill,
where we scattered our shoes and crumbs,
and took a nap on a grassy incline while the dog
kept an eye on the scraps of our meal. Your chin
glinted in the sun—evidence of an enthusiastic sip
of cider. A caterpillar caught my eye, hovering halfway
between clover stems, perhaps hiding from the mammoth
creatures dozing nearby, or perhaps he, too, needed to pause
and digest his dinner in the waning daylight.

Seed

I try to take a nap in your bed while you're at work.
I build myself a nest in clean, white linens
with a window for breath and a sliver of light.

Even here, in all this softness, the noise blooms
from within and without. The sun pulses
in hot ribbons on my skin between passing clouds.

I dream your hands into being. Here they appear,
curved around my curves, weight on my weight.
They wake me from my half-nap,
and I welcome the interruption.

First, I dream I am eating a croissant—
airy and buttery at its core,
with perfectly crisped layers.

Now, I *am* the croissant, and you are gently
peeling my pastry flakes open, biting
into my soft center.

Now, I am a rose, blooming upwards and outwards.
I feel the sensation of spreading and falling
as though the petals are my own limbs.

Now, I am a sea scallop, as wide as the plate it rests on,
with creamy white flesh. Simply a scallop, on its own,
without garnish, begging to be eaten.

Romance—true crime and beetle fungus

We celebrate each other's weirdness,
indulge the others' fixations, trying to listen
without judgment, no matter how disturbing the subject.

My October obsessions have a dark flavor,
predictable but no less intoxicating: vampires,
ghost stories, sociopaths and serial killers,
Ted Bundy, Jeffrey Dahmer, Andrew Cunanan
and their early childhoods in banal suburbia.

Your mania du jour is the mycelium
that grows under a beetle's exoskeleton,
Laboulbenia. You spend your Sunday in the lab
separating the microscopic mushrooms
from the carcass of a *Nebria* beetle
with miniature tweezers to extract the DNA,
while I spend time researching murderers
for some future graphic novel project.

This goes beyond listening and polite nods;
we even begin to adopt each other's vocational fervor.
I am slowly learning to identify Vermont ferns, your trade,
distinguishing characteristics of each species:
the grape fern, all alone on the side of the trail;
bracken fern, tall and logical; maidenhair fern,
elegant and well-rounded; polypody clinging to the rock;
wood fern growing in the shape of a vase; lady fern
with the extra fringed lace and dark skirts,
cinnamon fern with sharp teeth; interrupted fern
with softer lobes; hay-scented fern in the sunlit meadow;
royal fern, ample and spacious, set apart from the path.

While it has taken me a year or two to learn this simple list,
it does bring me delight and some dose of pride
to be able to participate in taxonomic dialogue with you,
my resident botanist. You too have expanded your interests
to reflect mine: you send me notable book reviews
and have added my favorite musical genre to your playlists:
female singer-songwriters with deep voices and word play,
and my film tastes are rubbing off on you; psychological
costume dramas about bisexual academics and artists.

Perhaps we'll switch: you'll write a novel about queer love
and intergenerational family drama, and I'll spend my days
pressing and drying liverworts and moss. Or we'll merge
into one supreme nerd, equal in our oddity and fervor.
Our bodies may begin to mold into similar shapes,
like Genesis P-Orridge and Lady Jaye, a pandrogyne union,
mirroring one another's expressions, genders, textures, passions.
Let's grow weird together, singing the same erratic tune.

Balance act

All stimuli meet at a busy intersection
between work and life—Michael juggles pans
and flips eggs in the kitchen—I see the rings
of sauce forming on the counter; knives balance
here and there, the stove begins to smoke. Breathe
and look away, I tell myself, while the dog
looks on, waiting for crumbs to drop,
as they always do, at Michael's feet.
The cat chases his own tail, which
he only recently discovered; round and round
he spins, both predator and prey in this eternal chase.

All the animals and animal-humans of the house blur;
limbs multiply in motion like a Muybridge photograph.

Where to sit? I shift books from one surface to another,
papers slide and pencils roll. Harriet's drawings
proliferate: cat comics, frog portraits, stick figures
of me, Michael, and her mom.

I try to hide my task list from myself; the to-dos
must wait. Here's a pen, just draw.

Soft / hard

I find a cat's claw embedded in my dog's ear:
a translucent half-moon, hidden in the furry crease
where her ear flops against her neck. How long
have you been holding this broken weapon, little one?

This evidence of a fight, are you the victor
or the vanquished? I too harbor shrapnel of battle
in my flesh—a thorn in my thumb from my encounter
with the honey locust in the woods this morning.

I hold you in my lap, whispering comforts
that you no longer need; what dog, after all, holds a grudge
or nurses the trauma of an hour passed? And while I rock you
in my lap, you keep your eyes fixed on the cottonwoods
which lean their limbs over the river, in case a squirrel
falls from a branch and lands in your mouth.

My eyes are trained not at the trees but the red rocks
beneath our feet. The shadows quiver, something
in the landscape shifts, and at first, I think *earthquake*
or *seizure*, but then I see the legs of hundreds of black spiders
dancing in and out of the cracks between stones.

I lift my hand to shield my eyes from the sun
and the shadow cast by my fingers sends the spiders into flight—
just like that, a whole village of arachnids disappears,
leaving me with holes in my vision:

the after-image spots and the spider nightmares I'll have tonight.
I pocket the cat's claw to remind me of the dangers lurking
just out of sight—behind your ear, under the skin of my thumb,
in the shadows between stones.

Stain

Stress manifests itself in tiny fiascos,
slapstick comedy without the humor:
I light the toaster on fire and carry it out
to the back step to smoke like some banished
houseguest with a cigarette habit. I forget about
the toaster and find it days later, rusting with rain.

In art class, my students take turns yelling "help!"
from various locations throughout the room:
by the sink, student A has too much paint on her hands
and struggles to turn on the faucet. Student B, legally blind,
is afraid to use the hot-glue gun, so I help her press the lever
and squish warm globules around her sculpture.
Strings of the dried glue tangle around her fingers
and I assure her there are no spider webs while I pluck
each thread from her hand. Student C needs
more papier mâché paste, immediately; student D
has spilled black paint all over her lap; student E
wants my advice about his abstract narwhal;
student F is experiencing a panic attack; student G
is slicing pencils in half with an exacto knife, and
on down the alphabet until the bell rings.

On the night of parent-teacher conferences,
I step on a tube of red paint—a big, fat, blood-colored
smear in the carpet in front of the art room door.
The headmaster walks by and shakes his head.

A bottle of seltzer explodes all over my pants
in the waiting room of the dentist, and I feel compelled
to tell the hygienist that I did not pee my pants.

One day mid-winter, mid-pandemic, mid-semester,
the wind is so vocal I can hear it through the walls
of the school, howling, screaming, snapping tree limbs
and displacing objects. On my way home from work,
I drive in a zig-zag to avoid all of the trash cans
and recycling bins that the wind tossed into the middle of the streets.
The wind's song blends with sirens and fighter jets overhead—
there's a military testing base nearby—it's hard to distinguish
each voice amidst this din. I try to reassure my dog
that everything is alright, everything will be alright,
but she doesn't speak my language. She spends
all night gazing up at me with soup-spoon eyes. I ask her,
"Who will pull the hot-glue strings from my fingers? Who will
mop the paint from my lap? Who will explain the sounds
of the wind?" She doesn't have any answers,
so I hold her curled up on my lap like a skein of yarn,
and I tell her all of the words I need to hear.

The Thinking Cup

The hand moves across the page of its own accord . . .
—Carolyn Forché

Visiting the parents of my partner—
I can't call them in-laws, we're not married,
there need to be more terms for modern relationships
when we don't fit into traditional unions—
I wake early to walk the dog. In the Back Bay,
there are many public alleyways and pocket gardens,
perfect for the dog to lift her leg on many a flower bed.

I find myself at the Thinking Cup, a cafe with
layers of history, and only one thin layer is mine.
I add to this memory with a new book of poetry
from the clearance shelf at the bookstore
down the street: Carolyn Forché's *Angel of History.*

I bought the book not for the angel on the cover,
but for the epigraph by Walter Benjamin,
from which Forché borrowed the title, about
Angelus Novus, a drawing by Paul Klee. The quote
is bleak, akin to the melancholic cycle of Sisyphus—
we repeat our mistakes, our brutality occurs eternally.

Here I sit, poised to begin reading with coffee in hand,
but the quiet is interrupted by a young and fancy couple
ardently discussing their mutual Catholicism.
It seems like a first date; they're too eager,

talking over one another, smiling to humor the other,
but not really listening. I flip through pages, gathering
scraps of poetry here and there. I read,
       "God's name *a boneless string of vowels...*"

I'm tempted to speak this verse aloud, to stir
the conversation of these pious could-be lovers.
She's wearing thick makeup and pearl earrings,
he absentmindedly fingers the gold cross on his neck,
while he mansplains "marriage" and "attachment."
The fruit tart on the table remains untouched,
perhaps as a symbol of their sexual virtue, their restraint.

I move outside to a table on the sidewalk, where
to my relief, the smattering of a dozen other customers
around me speak in languages not my own. Thus,
I have escaped from religious fanaticism, away from
the painfully awkward script of a Tinder date,
and melt into the cacophony of diverse linguistics
and pigeon antics. Now I can read this book of poems
in the open, irreverent air of the street.

Nabokov's ecstasy

An erasure of his "Butterflies" 1948

In the Russia of my boyhood, a swallowtail
made for the open window, soaring eastward,
over timber and tundra, to the Rocky Mountains—
to be overtaken on a dandelion after a forty-year race.

In my youth, I found herbariums in the attic
full of pressed edelweiss and maple leaves.

I felt the urge to explore the marshland
beyond the River Oredezh. In the pine groves
and alder scrub, bilberry shrubs with their dim,
dreamy blue fruit, I sought the perfume of butterfly wings
on my hands—vanilla, lemon, and musk.

Nature and art showed me the same enchantment
and deception— the magic intertwinkling facets
of entomological exploration. I used to sugar for moths
on my family's land—molasses, beer, and rum—
painted on tree trunks. On a boulder, a mountain ash
and an aspen had climbed, holding hands,
like two clumsy, shy children.

I have an acute desire to be alone. The older the man,
the queerer he looks with a butterfly net in his hand.
The lepidopterist has a special gentle awkwardness.
I find my own paradise in lupine, columbines, penstemons.

I do not believe in time. My ecstasy is a sense
of oneness with sun and stone. Butterflies and moths
are tender ghosts humoring this lucky mortal.
The ghost of purple under a moist young moon—
a hummingbird moth above a corolla.

Teasing the fibers apart

All morning we brew mulberry bark and the studio
fills with the smell of sweet rice pudding
with a touch of cardamom. We beat and pull
each fiber apart. Our thoughts and fingers
disintegrate into tubs of cold river water,
stained yellow with the dye of lotus leaves
that unfurl like the halos of frill-necked lizards.
The pulp soaks overnight in a tub with okra,
and in the morning we sift the clouds
onto fine screens, then flip the screens
over on blankets and mats. The water
seeps away, leaving thin skins of paper,
Which we gently drape on glass windows to dry.
The sheets hang in the sun, hinting
at the possibility of a future form: a book.

Ghost Brook

We call this place Ghost Brook
after the little white plant with no chlorophyl—
Monotropa uniflora, ghost pipe—
an ephemeral bloom which saps nutrients
from the roots of trees, semi-translucent,
like a rain-soaked mushroom stalk.

This is private property but we sneak in
at least once a month, to forage for mushrooms,
picnic by the frog pond, or to sit
on the wooden bench out on the peninsula.

There are other spirits here: the old farmhouses
submerged under the water's surface:
the man who drowned in shallow waters
a few years back when his feet gave way
on a slippery rock and he succumbed to water weeds.

Ghost-mimics haunt these woods; creatures who lurk
near the shore in white disguises: an egret, flying low;
an owl who hides in the marsh by the chanterelle patch.
These birds keep watch on the shapes above and below
the surface of the water: fish, insects, and humans.

Today, I am here practicing the ancient form
of photography, *cyanotypes,* or 'sun prints.'
I place squares of blue-green coated paper
on smooth stones and tenderly arrange
compositions of opaque objects: flowers, twigs,
moss, lichen, ferns, sand. These shapes

cast shadows; the green dye fades to yellow
as the sun burns their silhouettes into permanence.

I rinse the prints in a cold stream to develop the photos.
All that remains is the pale, white forms of plants—
afterimages of these fronds and petals—
botanical ghosts, painted in time.

Bloodroot

Sanguinaria canadensis

I know what you're after—
my eight-toothed crown of pearl and gold,
but if you tear my head at the neck
from wet spring clay
with your quick and greedy fingers,

I will give you only my torn stem
and stain your skin with ink.
I am a hemophiliac, a root whose blood
won't clot. Watch me expand into the fibers
of letters to unrequited loves. Even flower blood
turns brown. When my lobed leaves wither,

harvest my rhizome, dry it in the sunspot
on a sill. Brew a tea to numb your teeth.
I will stimulate your breath and fluids.
Sip me slowly or I'll make you bleed
for stealing my crown
before the peak of my blooming.

The skull

I found my place in the shade where the moss
is thick. The others can't see me; the ring of trees
and their shadows obscure my human form from view.

There's Bill, in the meadow by the amiable cow,
and over there is Angela, tracing the periphery
of the pond with her slow, graceful strides.
The rocking chairs on the porch look pleased
to be used, occupied by a contemplative poet.
Neil's under the chestnut with his sunhat akimbo.

In my personal sanctuary under the fir branches
and sugar maple canopies, I sense I'm being watched.
Not by the poets, but by some hidden presence:
a trickster sprite or a coven of holy toads.

Above my head dangles the skull of a creature.
Bobcat? Fox? Fisher? Possum? The skin
of the beast's face still clings to the bone,
gnarled and twisted with fine white whiskers.

Someone has decorated this glen as a dark chapel;
whether the skull is a sacrificial offering or a talisman
to keep spirits away, I can't be certain. The jaw has fallen
into the moss, and one sharp tooth points skyward,
waiting to pierce an unsuspecting foot. My feet
are booted and rest near the crushed shell of an egg.

A headless human form, sculpted in stone,
sits like a sentry guarding the forest. The body
is androgynous, strong, with hints of muscle,
alternately curved and flattened, like the torso
of a two-spirit warrior, or a genderless granite nymph.

Perhaps when I re-emerge from this uncanny glen,
I'll have aged through my youth like Rip Van Winkle,
and I will join the wise poets in the field.

While you're away

I swim over a shallow bed of zebra mussels, climb
halfway into the heart of a giant oak, gain two slivers
from an old, rotten dock, and sample a handful
of not-quite-ripe wild grapes. I visit an exhibit
of paper whales that hang like electric ghosts
from the ceiling, pulsing with light. I read a short story
about a little girl who finds a stone in the woods.
Every other line reminds me of you, so I hold the pen close
while I read. When I finish, the page looks
more like an ink painting, saturated in blue scribbles.

While you're away, I catalog flora and fauna specimens
to document and share with you from afar—
this is my love language—here, a dead bat in the grass,
its body transformed into mush by ants, but its wings
still intact, paper-thin translucence framed by delicate bones.
Here, a myriad of alien bodies: chanterelles in the moss,
puffballs on a log, and a choir of backlit oyster mushrooms
singing their spores into the wind. Here, a minuscule aphid
with fluorescent green skin and a spiked tail, bobbing up
and down on my notebook as though he's dancing for us.

While you're away, I find a cluster of glowworms in the dirt
on a night hike. I scoop the moist earth into my hands
to bring the light of these bioluminescent grubs
closer to my eyes. I want to share this vision with you. Instead,
I soak up their light and translate it into a story
to recount to you over a meal of smoked fish and fried peppers.
"Tell me again about the glowworms," you ask, and I will,
over and over until you can see them in your own hands.

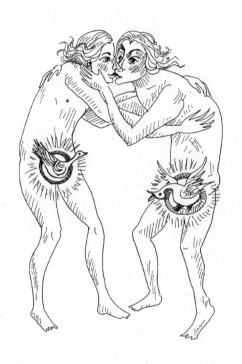

Acknowledgments

"While you're away" was selected as a finalist for the 2021 Poetry International Prize.

"Honey Hollow," "Wild orchids," and "Déjà vu" were published in Isele Magazine's online journal in 2022.

"Sagittaria" was published in a poetry anthology by Fifth Wheel Press in 2023.

"While you're away" and "Pounce" were included in the poetry anthology *Roads Taken: Contemporary Vermont Poetry,* 2021

Several of these poems have appeared in previous chapbooks, including *Sagittaria,* published by Bottlecap Press, *Predator Play,* by Ethel Zine, *Uranian Fruit,* by Honeybee Press, and *Image Burn,* self-published artist book.

Thank you to my attentive editors, including Dede Cummings, Meg Reynolds, Kate Baldwin, and Maria Tane. Thank you to Green Writers Press for all the behind-the-scenes work to bring this book into the world. Thank you as well to all the readers that helped advise me on earlier drafts of these poems, in workshop and beyond, including Meg (again), Duncan Campbell, Sam Hughes, Ben Aleshire, Skye Jackson, Robert McKay, and others. Thank you to Michael Sundue for your support and encouragement. Thank you to Sarah Diaz for the poetry prompts and inspiration. Thank you to the publishers of my poetry chapbooks and previous poetry collections that led to this book: Vagabond Press, Honeybee Press, Ethel Zine, and Bottlecap Press.

About the author

Frances Cannon is a writer, editor, educator, and artist. She is the Mellon Science and Nature Writing Fellow at Kenyon College, 2023 – 2025. She is an interdisciplinary writer, educator, editor, and artist whose work creatively combines prose and poetry with visual art into hybrid forms such as comics, graphic texts, and illustrated manuscripts. She teaches at Burlington City Arts and edits for Green Writers Press, Onion River Press, and Maple Tree Press. She recently served as the Managing Director of the Sundog Poetry Center in Vermont. She has taught at the Vermont College of Fine Arts, Champlain College, the Vermont Commons School, the University of Iowa, and as a visiting lecturer at Middlebury College and the University of Vermont. She has an MFA in creative writing from Iowa and a BA in poetry and printmaking from the University of Vermont. Her published books include *Walter Benjamin Reimagined,* MIT Press, *The Highs and Lows of Shapeshift Ma and Big-Little Frank,* Gold Wake Press, *Tropicalia,* Vagabond Press, *Predator/Play,* Ethel Press, *Uranian Fruit,* Honeybee Press, *Sagittaria,* Bottlecap Press, and *Image Burn,* a self-published art book, and *Fling Diction* (GWP 2024). She has worked for *The Iowa Review, McSweeney's Quarterly, The Believer,* and *The Lucky Peach.* Her writing has been published in *The New York Times, Poetry Northwest, The North American Review, The Iowa Review, The Green Mountain Review, Vice, Lithub, The Moscow Times, The Examined Life Journal, Gastronomica, Electric Lit, Edible magazine, North American Review, Fourth Genre, Rhino Poetry,* and *The Kenyon Review.*

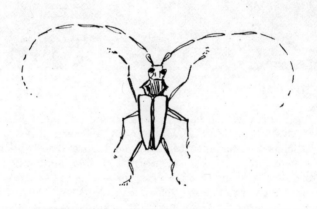